BRINGstorm

JOSH FARNWORTH

Copyright © 2019 Josh Farnworth.

All rights reserved. No part of this book may be reproduced, stored, or transmitted by any means—whether auditory, graphic, mechanical, or electronic—without written permission of the author, except in the case of brief excerpts used in critical articles and reviews. Unauthorized reproduction of any part of this work is illegal and is punishable by law.

ISBN: 978-1-6847-0183-4 (sc)
ISBN: 978-1-6847-0195-7 (e)

Library of Congress Control Number: 2019904432

Because of the dynamic nature of the Internet, any web addresses or links contained in this book may have changed since publication and may no longer be valid. The views expressed in this work are solely those of the author and do not necessarily reflect the views of the publisher, and the publisher hereby disclaims any responsibility for them.

This book is a work of non-fiction. Unless otherwise noted, the author and the publisher make no explicit guarantees as to the accuracy of the information contained in this book and in some cases, names of people and places have been altered to protect their privacy.

Any people depicted in stock imagery provided by Getty Images are models, and such images are being used for illustrative purposes only. Certain stock imagery © Getty Images.

Scripture taken from the King James Version of the Bible.

Lulu Publishing Services rev. date: 08/21/2019

For my parents,
Randy and Xanthe Farnworth
For my wife,
Carrie
And for my kids,
Bentley and Esther

I love you to the Death Star and back.

Acknowledgments

An epic thanks to my first and favorite editor, my mother, Xanthe. Your encouragement, insight, and expertise are irreplaceable. Thank you, Mom.

A special thanks to Lisa Thomas, the editor incredible, who molded this book into something worth reading. And to Ryan and Jessica Salmon for your friendship, feedback, and support.

Without any one of you, *Bringstorm* wouldn't be a reality.

"We are the music makers,
And we are the dreamers of dreams . . ."
— Arthur O'Shaughnessy, quoted by Willy Wonka

Preface

The way I understand it, new ideas are the by-product of thought collisions, those moments when unrelated experiences coalesce inside our brains. The birth of bringstorming wasn't any different: a few years ago, my experiences with a late-seventies Dodge Fireball and a typical brainstorming session collided in my noggin and the idea for bringstorming was born.

Let me explain. When I was growing up, my parents were the third—or maybe the fourth or fifth—owners of a 1979 Dodge Fireball motorhome, a cream-white, burnt-orange, and sulfur-yellow beast with a large bed over its cab and a surly 440-cubic-inch V8 motor nestled between its front seats. Looking at it from a distance, you'd probably guess it was just your average used motorhome, but it wasn't. It was special, extra special: in the fifteen-or-so years that my parents owned it, it only completed two of our family's annual summer road trips to grandma's without breaking down—two! Most of these breakdowns weren't typical either. On one trip, two tires blew within twenty miles of each other; on another, while exiting the freeway, the motorhome's rear bumper, with our ski boat hitched to it, broke off; and on another, because of a problem the motor was having, my dad had to run the carburetor with his right hand while steering the motorhome with his left. And at some point in almost every trip, the motorhome's air conditioning belt would snap and take all the other engine belts with it. Like I said, my parents' motorhome was extra special. Because of this, I spent countless hours on the interstate's shoulder in a sweat-soaked t-shirt and homemade shorts handing my dad different auto-parts and tools that, in his wisdom, he'd brought along. In all our years of traveling with this motorhome, we never had to call a mechanic, a tow truck, or AAA. Dad just always came prepared with whatever we needed to fix the day's breakdown, which brings me to the point of this first experience: from a young age, I learned to be prepared.

Dad, you're the man.

Fast forward twenty-five years or so. While participating in a group brainstorm, I noticed something about myself. I was having a difficult time spontaneously generating innovative ideas. I, the art director on the project, literally couldn't think of anything to contribute. I surveyed the group and noticed that other people seemed to be having the same problem. As I sat through the brainstorm, hoping no one would notice that I had contributed diddly-squat and worrying that my creative spark had burned out forever, I took a mental step back and thought about why my teammates and I were having trouble. Suddenly, my past motorhome experiences and my current brainstorming experience collided, touching off a series of questions inside my head. What if instead of showing up with a by-the-seat-of-my-pants attitude, I brought a few ideas to share and collaborate about? What if everyone, like my dad, showed up prepared? How would that change the process? How would it improve the results? What if everyone in the group brought ideas to share? Then it hit me: What if we had a *bringstorm?*

■ ■ ■

You may have noticed, as I have, that brainstorming doesn't always work. Now, I'm not devaluing brainstorming. Like every other creative tool, it has its uses. In my experience, brainstorming is an excellent tool to use if you want to get a group to loosen up, if you need to produce a large amount of wild ideas, or if you need to encourage creativity and excitement during a project. However, over the course of my career, I have also become aware of brainstorming's limitations. First, brainstorms don't encourage preparation. Second, they don't guarantee individual investment: I've participated in many brainstorm sessions where only a few members of the group participated. And third, while brainstorms produce volumes of ideas, many of the ideas they produce miss their intended target. Because of these flaws, I realized that a different creative tool was needed, and that's half of the reason I developed bringstorming.

The other half of my motivation, and the reason I wrote *Bringstorm*, came a few years ago when I was working at a local museum. While I was walking through the museum's lobby, a guest approached me, asked me some questions, and then asked me for directions. After answering her questions and showing her where she needed to go, I had an epiphany. I realized that I enjoy helping people find their way. That little experience inspired me to figure out how I could help people find their way on a larger scale. Shortly after helping that guest, I realized that lots of individuals and organizations get lost in the creative process, and I saw that I had the skills and experience to help them find their way through it. So that's why I developed the bringstorm process, wrote this book, and now facilitate bringstorm workshops.

I hope you find bringstorming to be as helpful and effective as I have. I'm confident you will.

Introduction

It's surprising how many individuals and organizations unconsciously adopt a show-up-and-see-what-happens approach to creativity and problem solving. While showing up is a good thing, simply hoping for innovative and useful ideas to "happen" isn't a reliable recipe for success. The best chefs collect the ingredients they need *before* they cook. Get my drift? So rather than falling for the quasi-collaboration and catered lunch that accomplishes nothing because no one comes prepared, let me introduce bringstorming.

Foundationally, bringstorming is about one thing: coming to meetings prepared with ideas to share. Just like a master chef brings ingredients to cook with, each member of a bringstorm team brings ideas to collaborate about, and this makes a massive difference. Now, I realize that showing up to meetings with ideas to share isn't a new concept. For some professionals, it's second nature; however, for many, it isn't. Until now, the process that many successful professionals use to prepare and present winning ideas has remained nameless, underdeveloped, and overlooked. With *Bringstorm,* I hope to share an organized, preparation-based approach to collaborative creativity that anyone can follow to generate, evaluate, and develop truly good ideas.

About now, you might be asking: does bringing ideas to share really make that big of a difference in creative collaboration? Yes! During my career, I've seen how this seemingly minor adjustment in the way individuals and organizations approach creativity transforms their creative output from mediocre to exceptional. But bringing ideas to share isn't the only ingredient in bringstorming's recipe for creative success. In this book, I'll share other tips as well.

The first three chapters cover how to define your project's purpose, explore ideas alone, and test ideas using simulations and prototypes. I'll show how to

- stay true to your project's original intent so that you solve the problem you set out to solve,
- explore alone to allow yourself greater creative freedom (it's more comfortable to make mistakes in private), and
- build rough and function-focused prototypes to expose and resolve idea-blind-spots.

In chapters four, five, and six, I'll give you the "how to" of bringstorm meetings. You'll learn how to

- create bringstorm pages and use them to retain ideas,
- run bringstorm meetings that encourage meaningful team contribution and collaboration, and
- rate ideas presented during bringstorm meetings to identify optimal solutions and retain good ideas.

In chapters seven, eight, and nine, I'll discuss the benefits of creating and maintaining a bringstorm library, the importance of repeating the bringstorm process until you've discovered a winning idea, and what the path to success really looks like (hint: it's not straight). And finally, in the appendix I've made a quick-reference guide containing resources and examples for you to use and peruse on the fly.

What's the Difference Between *Bring*storming and *Brain*storming?

Whenever I introduce someone to the concept of bringstorming, a common question I get asked is, "What's the difference between a ***bring***storm and a ***brain***storm?" The short answer is preparation. The long answer requires a little more explanation. To explain how these two creative tools are different, let's look first at what **brain**storming is, and then compare it with **bring**storming.

Brainstorming

Typically, when people say "let's have a brainstorm," they are saying "let's meet, put our heads together, and see if we can pull some big ideas or innovative solutions out of thin air." And while this isn't exactly the way that brainstorms are meant to work (proper brainstorms are guided by a specific set of rules), it's generally how they're done. If you'd like to learn more about the rules of brainstorming and how to apply them, read Tom Kelley's book *The Art of Innovation*. It's an excellent brainstorming guide.

Because the brainstorm process is often misunderstood and misapplied, I categorize brainstorms in one of two ways: bad ones or good ones (revolutionary categories, I know). Bad brainstorms are counterfeit-creative meetings that are used as a last resort—a project is fizzling, so the people involved get together to discuss why and rehash old ideas about how to make it sizzle again. These kinds of brainstorms are generally uninspiring and fruitless. Good brainstorms are genuine creative meetings that are used to change perspectives, connect minds, and generate lots of wild and hopefully wonderful ideas. These kinds of brainstorms are generally inspiring and fruitful, but they aren't always; sometimes a good brainstorm session can flop. To quote Kurt Vonnegut Jr., "So it goes."

Bringstorming

While brainstorming is often an effective creative tool, it isn't the only one or always the best one to use. That's why I'm sharing another excellent creative tool: **bring**storming. Bringstorming is different from brainstorming in one major way: everyone prepares ideas to share and collaborate about. Unlike a brainstorm meeting in which a group shows up, states the problem, and then generates and connects random or spur-of-the-moment ideas to discover innovative solutions to problems, bringstorming involves defining your purpose in advance, exploring alone, preparing, and *then* sharing and collaborating about the ideas that have been brought.

For me, when thinking of the difference between bringstorming and brainstorming, it's helpful to compare bringstorming to a laser and brainstorming to a light bulb: bringstorming focuses ideas on a single goal, while brainstorming freely radiates ideas that may or may not be on target. With the different applications of lasers and lightbulbs in mind, remember that bringstorms aren't meant to replace brainstorms. Feel free to use both bringstorming and brainstorming together. Both are useful tools for generating and discovering great ideas. If, while collaborating during a bringstorm meeting, you'd like to brainstorm about an idea that's been shared, go for it. There's no reason not to. Over the past twelve-or-so years, I've spent a lot of time as a product designer and as an art director for children's museums, and, during that time, I've used both bringstorming and brainstorming (often together) to create successful products and experiences, and I suggest you do too.

How Bringstorming Helps Individuals and Teams

Bringstorming helps individuals and teams create better products and processes because it encourages preparedness, keeps creativity on target, and guarantees individual investment. It eliminates loss aversion, reveals idea-blind spots, promotes equality, encourages respectful collaboration, and provides a simple system to retain and organize ideas.

During my career, I've seen how bringstorming improves group dynamics, individual attitudes, and results. A few years ago while I was working as an art director for a museum, the department I was working in frequently held brainstorm sessions that typically went like this: everyone in the group would show up idealess, the brainstorm would begin, some members of the group would participate while others pretended to, we would come up with whiteboards full of ideas, pick the idea or ideas we liked the best, and then everyone would go on their merry way. Well, everyone except me, whose job it was to take the rough ideas we'd come up with and turn them into something reasonable and buildable. After being stuck with this assignment for a while, I decided I'd had enough. So I developed and implemented the bringstorm, and the whole experience changed: everyone came prepared with ideas, shared them, collaborated, and left with a clear understanding of the product or process that was being created. And, as needed, team members were involved in the process of production and implementation. Because I had implemented bringstorming, I was no longer the lone brain assigned to make order out of chaos: I had an informed and invested team to help me.

If you or your team is struggling to come up with innovative ideas, meet deadlines and client expectations, or deliver products or processes that are on target, try bringstorming. It works wonders.

If it Works for Dr. Feynman. . .

Recently, I read the book *Surely You're Joking Mr. Feynman* written by the renown physicist Dr. Richard P. Feynman, who, during World War II, worked with other extraordinary scientists—"great men" as he calls them—to develop the atomic bomb. The scientists he worked with included Arthur Compton, Richard Tolman, Henry Smyth, Harold Urey, Isidor Rabi, and J. Robert Oppenheimer. While developing the bomb, Dr. Feynman and the previously mentioned scientists belonged to an evaluation committee that had to figure out the best way to separate uranium into different isotopes. For several reasons, this was a difficult problem to solve. Lucky for you and me though, in his book, Dr. Feynman gives a glimpse into the process they used to find a solution. The committee would get together and discuss the problem. It's safe to assume that, like most scientists, they spent some time in their labs researching potential solutions before coming to the group meeting to present their ideas. Then, during the group discussion, one scientist would share his ideas for solving the problem and debate the idea with the rest of the group, and then another scientist would present another idea to solve the same problem, and they would debate that one, and so on. After a period of exploration through constructive argument, the committee's chairman would choose the idea that he thought was the best, and the team would pursue it.

This example demonstrates the value in the approach these scientists used to solve problems and generate ideas.

If the greatest minds solve problems by bringing, sharing, and discussing ideas, we should too.

So if you learn one lesson from this book, let it be this: bring ideas to share.

With that said, let's get on with it. Let's bringstorm.

1

Define Your Purpose

"Begin with the end in mind." —Stephen Covey

Defining your project's purpose gives you an anchor to tie to and explore from, just like an anchor does in rock climbing.

I made this connection last year when, after some coaxing, I convinced my eleven-year-old son Bentley, who has a fear of heights, to try rock climbing. To ensure his first climbing experience was a positive one, I took him to a local climbing gym, and, before I knew it, Bentley and I were standing at the base of his first climb: a forty-five-foot wall with a reinforced-steel anchor extruding from its top. Looped around the anchor was a thick nylon rope, whose ends touched the floor near our feet. Picking up both ends of the rope, I attached one end to my harness and the other to Bentley's. As I did, I explained to him that because both of us were attached to the anchor, he didn't need to worry about falling. A short time later he reached the top of the wall, gave me a big smile, a thumbs up, and rappelled down. Because he and I were both attached to the anchor, he climbed without the fear of falling; I relaxed, confident he was safe, and we enjoyed our experience.

Inventing new products or processes, coming up with innovative ideas, and finding solutions to problems can feel like rock climbing when you're afraid of heights: intimidating. To suppress feelings of intimidation, add direction, and give purpose to any project, I suggest anchoring it. Just like rock climbers use anchors to stay safely on course, we can keep our ideas on course by anchoring them to our purpose. So how do we connect ideas to our purpose? Define our purpose and then evaluate our ideas with our defined purpose in mind.

How to Define Your Project's Purpose

The first step in every creative endeavor is to anchor your project by defining its purpose, usually by figuring out what problem you're solving, what product or process you're improving, what you're creating, and why. I realize that taking the time to define your project's purpose might seem tedious or unnecessary, but having a clear understanding of why you're working on a project and what you're going to accomplish is indispensable. Moving forward without it is like rock climbing without equipment: it's risky. And while using a willy-nilly approach to creativity won't kill you, it often leaves you chasing tangents (pursuing ideas that won't work), or even worse, it can kill your project. So take the time define your projects purpose. Take the time to anchor it.

Sometimes a project's purpose is obvious and defining it is straightforward, while sometimes your purpose isn't so obvious. In either case, to help you identify and define your project's purpose, I suggest you have a "DDQ." DDQ stands for "discuss, define, and question." A DDQ, like a BBQ, is a relaxed meeting between team members, or, if you're working solo, it's a meeting with a colleague who, if possible, is knowledgeable about what you're working on. In either case, discuss, define, and question the project's purpose. Here are the steps of an effective DDQ:

1. Gather your team (you and a larger group or you and one other person).
2. **Discuss** your project. Talk about *why* you want to do the project and *what* you're going to do. Set a goal. As you discuss, here's a list (feel free to add to it) of questions that you can use to discover your purpose:

    a. Why are we pursuing this project? (Pssst, money shouldn't be the only reason.)
    b. How does this project add value?

c. What product or process are we going to create or improve?
   d. What problem are we going to solve?
   e. What is our goal?

3. **Define** your project by writing a purpose statement. A purpose statement is a clear and accurate definition of why you're going to do a project and what you're going to do. For reference, a purpose statement should be structured like Simon Sinek suggests in his TED Talk "Start with Why": Because ___(why)___, we are going to ___(what)___. The why is followed by the what. Here's an example: Because we love children and hate to see them cry when adhesive bandages are removed, we are going to create a gentle adhesive for children's bandages.

4. **Question** your definition. Once you've discussed and defined your purpose, take the third step and *question* your definition. Ask, "if we stay true to our purpose statement, will we accomplish our goal?" If the answer is yes, then congratulations! You've anchored your project. If the answer is no, repeat steps one and two.

How to Stick to Your Project's Defined Purpose

If you're shooting a crumpled paper into the wastebasket near your desk, being off by a few degrees doesn't matter much. But if you're piloting the space shuttle from Cape Canaveral to the moon, and your trajectory is off by one degree, you'll miss the moon by over four thousand miles! Yikes and sayonara! Which brings me to my point: small changes in direction can either keep a project on target or turn it into space dust.

As strange as it seems, it's easy to begin developing say, the greatest pair of shorts of all time, and end up developing pants. Creative projects are wildly susceptible to subtle changes in direction—a new team member joins the team and bumps things slightly off course with an uninformed opinion, a manager drops in to see how things are going and steers the project in a new direction with a "better" idea of his or her own, or an idea you love doesn't connect to the project's purpose but you pursue it anyway—capiche?

So as you and your team members create new products or processes, generate new ideas, or find solutions to problems, periodically take a few minutes to evaluate your direction. Ask the following question: if we keep doing what we're doing, will we fulfill our purpose?

Now you might be asking, "What if, at some point in

the project, we evaluate it and discover that it has become disconnected from its purpose? How do we reconnect it?" Here's how:

1. Stop moving forward with the project.
2. Retrace your steps. Review the work that's been done until you find the point of departure (the idea, suggestion, email, etc. that disconnected the project from its purpose).
3. Resume working on the project from the point of departure.

Last year my parents gave me the Lego Technic Rally Car set for Christmas—yes, I'm in my late thirties, and I still enjoy putting LEGOs together. And yes, my parents give me and my mid-thirties brother (I'm not the only weirdo in the family) a LEGO set every Christmas. It's tradition! Anyway, last Christmas, after building two major components of the rally car, I tried to connect them, and it didn't work. The pegs didn't line up with the holes. As much as I enjoy putting LEGOs together, I wasn't excited to retrace my steps, dismantle a major part of the rally car, and then correctly reassemble it, but I did it anyway. While it took some time to work backwards through the instructions, identify my point of departure, and dismantle and rebuild the component, it was worth it. Sooner than I expected, the build was back on track. As homegrown and hokey as this example is, it illustrates how to reconnect a project to its purpose without completely starting over.

However, retracing your steps and restarting at the point of departure isn't always the right choice. Sometimes, even though it can be more difficult, it is better to start over.

Have the Courage to Start Over

That's right. Sometimes we need to admit that a product or process we've been working on wasn't tied to the project's purpose from the very beginning.

For example, during my junior year in college, I was building a 3D computer model for one of my design classes, and it wasn't going well. Hours of frustration and struggle passed until finally I gave up and admitted to myself that I'd spawned a 3D-model-from-hell. Discouraged, I showed my professor the model I'd built and told him that no matter what I did, my model only seemed to get worse, to get more complex. After looking over my work, my professor turned to me, and said: "start over."

When I told him I didn't want to start over, he promised me that if I did, I would be able to build a new model in about a third of the time. I hesitated, then gathered my courage, trashed my model, and began again. And I discovered that my professor was right. In a third of the time it took to build a 3D-model-from-hell, I'd built a simple and accurate model.

When I believed that my failed first attempt was a waste of time, my professor knew better. He knew that the knowledge I gained from my failure had equipped me for success. So when you realize you need to start a project over, don't be frustrated with yourself or your team or fret about having wasted time, energy, and money. Like Aubrey de Grey says, "don't cling to a mistake just because you spent a lot of time making it." Instead, remember that starting over is a step forward that will not only stop you from spending more time, energy, and money on a doomed idea, but it will also allow you to restart the project with more experience.

One more thing you can do to ease the pain of having to start over is to salvage the work you've done: pick out the good ideas, create bringstorm pages for them (see chapter 4), and save them inside the bringstorm library (see chapter 7). Then, reconnect with the project's purpose, and start over.

▪ ▪ ▪

Accurately defining your purpose and then remaining faithful to it will help you and your team pursue great ideas that connect to your project's purpose and temporarily retreat from great ideas that don't connect. In summary, sometimes it's downright tempting to kick off a project without taking the time to get a solid understanding of what its true purpose is. Resist this temptation. Begin every project by defining its purpose, and, as it progresses, evaluate your work to make sure it connects to that purpose. If you do, you'll be glad you did. If you don't—good luck, Chuck.

Chapter Summary

- Have a DDQ—discuss, define, and question your purpose.
- Write a purpose statement.
- Stay true to your project's original purpose by regularly evaluating its direction and starting over if necessary.
- Be wary of seemingly insignificant changes in a project's direction.

2

Explore Ideas Alone

"Be alone, that is the secret to invention; be alone, that is when ideas are born." — Nikola Tesla

For me, and I'm guessing a lot of other people, it can be difficult to spontaneously generate valuable ideas or innovative solutions to problems. And it can be even more difficult when you're expected to produce these ideas or solutions with the CEO or your crush from marketing or the company nay-sayer in the room. For a myriad of reasons, when other people are present, most of us behave differently than we would if we were alone: we play it safe, we're more reserved, we're extra polite, we defer to others' experience over our own, etc. Because of this, I believe we are the most creative when we are free—free from social pressure, company culture, and the controversial opinions of others.

Inhibition impedes exploration—remove it! Explore ideas alone (at least at first).

When we take time to explore alone in an environment without social repercussion, we're free to fail and succeed privately. Being free to explore ideas uninhibited helps us relax, focus, and enter a state often referred to as *flow*, a state in which ideas stream through us seemingly without effort. So break away from the group, retreat to your creative space, turn off, mute, silence, ignore, and/or forward any gizmos that will inevitably distract you, slap a "do not disturb" sign on your door, and start exploring.

What Exploring Alone Looks Like

Spending time alone solving problems and generating ideas is my favorite part of the bringstorm process. It's my *free* time, time I get to work, explore, and innovate freely and without interference. When I explore alone, I go to my office (my creative space), close the door, and surround myself with my tools (computer, paper, pens, markers, books, magazines, and movies). Then, I make up a title for the project and write it in bold letters at the top of a sheet of paper (an ideation page, more on these in a moment), and, with the project's purpose in mind, I start exploring. I search the internet, books, magazines, images, and movies for ideas and inspiration. When I get an idea from a website, a chapter or article, an image, or a video, I add it to my ideation page by writing the idea down and sketching it. And when I feel like I've found a first-rate idea, I not only write it down and sketch it, but I also prototype it (see Chapter Three). Often, in addition to writing, sketching, and prototyping my ideas, I'll make a note about where I found the information that inspired the idea, so I can find it again. While that might seem like a trivial thing to do, I've found it to be a helpful habit, helpful because I can easily share the sources of my ideas with others and reorient myself with a project when I get interrupted.

Having shared the process I use when I explore alone, I'd better mention that your process will be different than mine, and that's a good thing because different processes produce different ideas. So when you spend time exploring alone, do it your way. However, I do recommend you adopt the following three habits:

1. explore in an environment that promotes creativity, focus, and personal freedom;
2. record your ideas and sources of inspiration on ideation pages; and
3. surround yourself with tools that will help you explore efficiently.

Speaking of tools, in addition to computers, books, magazines, movies, paper, pens, and markers, some other tools you can use to find inspiration are places: the great outdoors, fabrication shops, city parks, museums, colleges, and hardware stores are excellent places to find ideas.

∎ ∎ ∎

In Chapter One, I mentioned that pursuing tangents can kill projects. While that's true for the project as a whole—you don't want to solve a different problem than the one you set out to solve—following tangents when you're exploring alone is encouraged. But be aware that you have to police yourself. If you've been exploring a tangent for a while and aren't finding ideas or getting inspiration, move on. To avoid unproductive tangents and stay on course, I keep the project's purpose in mind as I explore, and I pay close attention to my creative instincts. If my instincts tell me watching a third cat video on YouTube or reading more about narwhal migratory patterns isn't going to lead me to new ideas or inspire me, I mentally reconnect with the project's purpose and explore something new. That might sound like hocus pocus, but it isn't; you know when you're actively seeking ideas and solutions and when you're wasting time.

Ideation Pages

While relying on your creative instincts to guide you as you explore is important, keeping track of your ideas and where they came from is important too. The best way I've found to keep track of my ideas as I explore is by creating what I call *ideations pages*. Ideation pages are quick and dirty records of your creative journey, a mishmash of notes and sketches that you'll organize later (see Chapter Four and the Appendix for examples). Keep in mind that the ideation pages you create are *just for you*. You don't have to share them or show them to anyone unless you want to. Make them *yours*, fearlessly fill them with elementary level sketches, imperfectly punctuated notes, and grease stains from cookie crumbs.

As you use ideation pages to record your creative journey, you'll find they are great tools for rapid idea generation and retention, and that they also serve a less obvious purpose: they help eliminate another form of inhibition called loss aversion. Loss aversion is a term used in economics to describe what happens when a person chooses to avoid a loss over realizing an equivalent gain. In creative pursuits, loss aversion happens when people stop exploring because they've found an idea they love and are afraid to lose it, adapt it, or change it. Use ideation pages to ease the fear of forgetting or losing an idea: write it down or make a quick sketch of it or do both, and then keep exploring with confidence. And when you're finished, you'll be surprised by the number of innovative ideas you've discovered, ideas you'll be chomping at the bit to share.

To Explore Better, Relax

The actor and comedian Bill Murray says that "the more relaxed you are, the better you are at everything: the better you are with your loved ones, the better you are with your enemies, the better you are at your job, the better you are with yourself." Having a relaxed and happy attitude toward any stage of a project (even the ones we initially dread) makes the entire experience more enjoyable. If you're exploring ideas for a project that you're not thrilled about or one that has a nail-biting timeline, here are some steps to help you enjoy the process (at least most of the time):

1. Relax. Take a deep breath if you need to, release it, and clear your mind. Put the anger from your commute or your concerns about the upcoming zombie apocalypse on hold.
2. Focus your thoughts on the project. This can be difficult, especially on sunny spring days, the week before a vacation, or Friday afternoons. But you've

got to do it. Here are some short-term and long-term things you can do to focus:

- *Short Term:* Turn off or silence any electronic devices that will distract you; politely ask others not to disturb you and tell them why you don't want to be disturbed; work in bursts, work for short amounts of time focusing only on the project; before you begin to work on a project, do a few jumping jacks, stretch, or do a few power poses; don't overeat before you need to focus; and finally, do eat some dark chocolate (scientists have proven it enhances focus—thank you scientists).
- *Long Term:* Exercise regularly, eat healthy foods, get the right amount of sleep, don't overwork, and regularly review your reasons for doing the project—think of the value it will bring to others and the value it will bring to you.

3. Find an element of the project that interests you, some glint inside the perceived darkness that catches your eye, and start exploring from there. For example, if you're not excited about redesigning a toaster, find something related to toasters that does excite you, like electricity or the plastic molding process or the

physics of springs, or whatever, and explore that—let your creative intuition guide you. Whenever possible, relax, have fun, and enjoy the flow.

■ ■ ■

The bringstorm process is meant to be fun and thought provoking. If you've enjoyed exploring and you're excited to share what you discovered, you'll find that the other members of your team will be eager to see and hear about what you've found. So be enthusiastic and share the ideas that you're genuinely excited about. Don't share an idea because you think it will impress your manager or inspire desire in your office crush or show your intellectual prowess. Be genuine: explore and share ideas that add value and momentum to the project.

Chapter Summary

- Remove inhibition by exploring alone.
- Surround yourself with helpful tools.
- Let your creative intuition guide you.
- Record ideas and useful notes on ideation pages.
- Relax, focus, and let the ideas flow.

3

Testing

"Fail faster; succeed sooner." — *David Kelley*

Testing an idea reveals its flaws and strengths. As we develop ideas for products and processes inside our brains, those ideas often appear flawless to our mind's eye, and this can lead to "idea blind-spots," or flaws in our ideas that we don't see. So why don't we see them? Because ideas are born inside our minds, they begin life in a hypothetical state, a state that isn't subject to physical laws, like gravity and motion; to the constraints of physical materials, like plywood and plastic; or to immaterial factors like emotions, expectations, and relationships. We can think about how gravity will affect our idea; about how using plywood may be beneficial; or about how changing a customer service process, sales pitch, or return policy will make customers happier, but we don't know what affect any one of these will have until we test it.

Simply claiming that an idea will improve a product or a process leaves a lot of room for doubt. But backing up a claim with a successful real-world test makes it hard to deny that it will work. Testing ideas to give them credibility is an important part of the bringstorm process. If you, your team, or your client is struggling to believe that an idea will work, test it. It's the best and fastest way to reveal an idea's blindspots and prove its strengths.

When to Test

Testing should be done throughout a project. At any point in the bringstorm process, you are free to test an idea. When you are exploring alone, test an idea by building quick and simple prototypes, and then bring both your idea and your prototypes to the bringstorm meeting. If during the bringstorm meeting, the group wants to test an idea that has been shared by simulating it, do it. And after the bringstorm meeting, frequently test a winning idea to explore, refine, and improve it. You be the judge: if you feel the need to test a product or a process at any point, go for it.

Types of Ideas

Generally, I assign ideas to one of three categories: product ideas, process ideas, and mixed product and process ideas, what I simply call *mixed ideas*. Ideas for physical products are built out of physical materials. Ideas for immaterial processes are built through simulation. And mixed ideas require a physical prototype to test a process.

How to Test Ideas for Physical Products

Ideas for physical products are tested by building prototypes out of materials like wood, metal, paper-mache, clay, Styrofoam, your co-worker's shoelaces, LEGOs, paperclips, etc. They work wonders for artists, designers, fabricators, architects, and engineers—people who create physical objects or systems. Now, I'm guessing that the process for developing and testing physical ideas is obvious: you have an idea for a physical product, do some preliminary work, build a prototype like the one pictured below, and then test it.

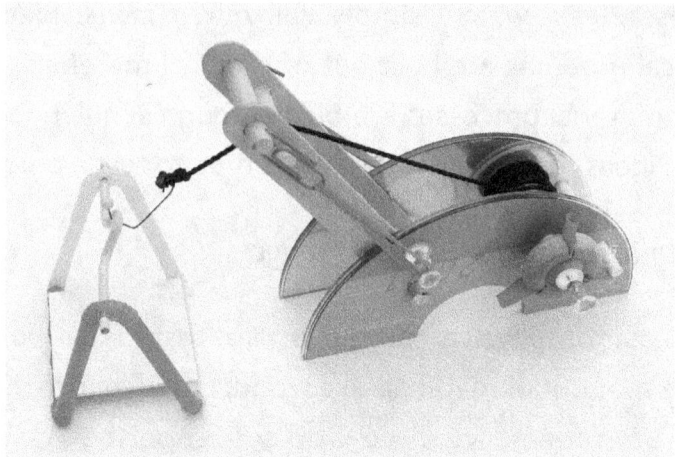

Simple prototypes made from everyday items, like the crane prototype pictured above, can help reveal an idea's strengths and weaknesses before a major investment of time and money is made.

As a product designer, I've built and tested hundreds of prototypes. Every time I've built and tested a prototype, I've learned more about the product I'm designing, more about what's working and what isn't. If you want to create successful physical products, build and test lots of prototypes.

How to Test Ideas for Processes

Ideas for processes are tested through simulation by physically going through the steps and motions of a process or by writing them down. Simulations work wonders for CEOs., managers, sales people, teachers, and the like—people who create immaterial things like company cultures, customer experiences, business relationships, and environments for learning.

To show you how to test an idea for a process, here's a hypothetical example: pretend, for a moment, that you're a sales manager that's been asked to *improve customer service at your company's sales counter*. Here's what you should do:

1. Observe, evaluate, and participate in the existing process.
2. Bringstorm a new (or improved) process by following the steps outlined in previous and upcoming chapters in this book.
3. Simulate the new process. Round up your sales team, go down to the customer service counter, and roleplay it. That's right—lose your inhibitions and find your courage, because simulation often requires a little acting. And don't just simulate it once; do it as many times as you need to, swapping roles with team members, and improving it as you go. Once you and your team are confident that the new process works better than the old one, test it further by trying it with actual customers.

A few years ago, the director of interactive exhibits for a local museum and a friend and colleague of mine, Dave Stroud, went through this very process:

1. Dave observed that the members of his staff were doing a superficial job maintaining the museum's exhibits. Instead of meticulously evaluating the exhibits external and internal components (cases, locks, buttons, wiring, motors, bearings, computers, etc.), they would casually inspect them and consider their job done. To inspire his staff to do a better job, Dave offered them small financial rewards for better inspections, but it didn't work.
2. After exploring ideas about how to improve maintenance and incentivize his staff, Dave's solution was to hide tiny plastic unicorns inside the exhibits, where they would be found only if the maintenance staff did a thorough job. When a staff member found a unicorn, they would bring it back to Dave for a reward. Dave met with his staff, explained his "find-the-unicorn" idea, and invited them to each choose an individual reward for finding a unicorn during their exhibit maintenance.
3. Shortly after explaining his idea to his team, Dave simulated the new method. He hid some unicorns

inside a few exhibits and asked his staff to look for them as they did their daily maintenance. It worked. His staff paid closer attention to their work and spent more time evaluating and looking over the individual components of each exhibit. After proving that the "find-the-unicorn" process would work, Dave hid unicorns in exhibits throughout the museum: maintenance improved, and everyone received a reward they were excited about.

How to Test Mixed Ideas

A mixed idea combines a physical product with a process, or, in other words, a mixed idea typically requires a physical or digital prototype to be built in order to run an accurate simulation. For example, a detective mocks up a crime scene to simulate how a crime was committed or an architect makes a 3D computer model of an entryway to simulate the flow of foot traffic through it or firefighters use a simulated-structural-fire building to practice putting out fires. These kinds of ideas, because of their hybrid nature, can be found in every profession.

To show you what testing a mixed idea looks like, here's an example I found while watching the movie *The Founder*. In the movie, the McDonald brothers needed to find a way to make their restaurants' kitchens more efficient.

To accomplish this, they went to a local tennis court and drew the layout of their kitchen using chalk. In the layout, they included every prep-station and piece of equipment. Then they brought their employees to the tennis court, distributed them on the drawing (their prototype), and had them simulate making and handing out food orders. After watching their employees bump into and stumble over each other, the McDonald brothers moved the employees to the side, erased the old layout, drew a new one, and ran the simulation again. After repeating this process many times, the McDonald brothers found the most efficient way to layout their restaurants' kitchens, and voila! The fast-food industry was born.

Levels of Idea Development for Testing

Now, the McDonald brothers could have spent years and hundreds of thousands of dollars physically rebuilding their restaurants' kitchens over and over again to test different layouts, but they didn't. Instead, they combined simple, or what I call "research-quality" prototypes with basic simulations to solve their problem and saved themselves a hefty amount of time, money, and stress.

This is a crucial lesson to learn when testing ideas: don't overdevelop an idea before testing it. Ideas can be developed to many different levels. These levels range from research quality (quick, rough, and cheap) to display quality (slow, refined, and expensive). And all of them have their place; however, for bringstorming, I recommend research-quality tests. Why? Because these simpler tests are quick, inexpensive, and easily built from resources you have on hand: paper, rubber bands, LEGOs, phone cameras, basic acting, and chalk drawings on a tennis court.

Another reason I recommend focusing on research-quality tests is that they keep projects flowing. Many projects stagnate when individuals and groups focus too much energy on creating display-quality tests when rough ones will do. I'd rather spend twenty minutes and a few dollars to expose idea-blind spots than the alternative, and I bet you would too. To see an example of a display-quality test (slow, refined, and expensive) that turned out to be a waste of time, check out this mini-washing machine prototype that I built years ago:

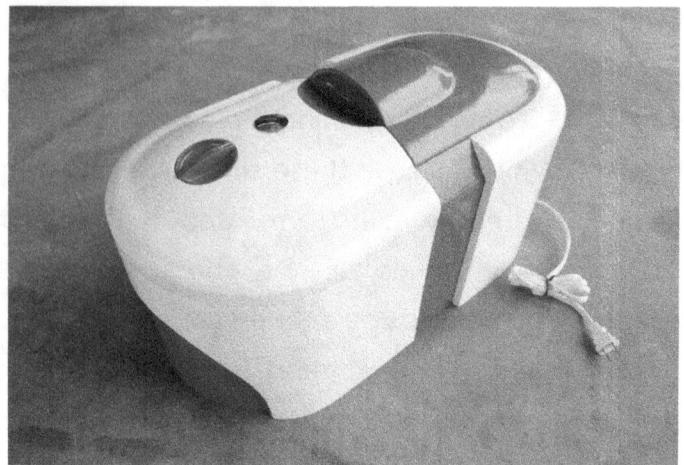

Creating a display-quality test (a mini-washing machine prototype in this case) is a waste of time and resources when a research-quality test will do.

Now, you might be saying to yourself, "this looks like a great prototype to me." As far as looks go, you'd probably be right; however, it was a dud. Here's why: after three weeks of work, I discovered that it was too small. That's right; I spent three weeks building a display-quality prototype when I could have made the same discovery using a fifteen-minute-research-quality prototype. Shame on me. So unless you are creating a final process or product to present to a client or are creating something for public display, focus on testing research quality prototypes and simulations. This may mean you build a prototype with odds and ends from your desk (like the toy crane pictured earlier), or you simulate a process by filming your sales team roleplaying at a conference table turned "customer service counter" rather than investing in a full-scale training film complete with narration, professional lighting, and well-rehearsed demonstrations. For bringstorming purposes, keep it simple.

Ideas Are for Sharing

Figuring out what works and what doesn't is part of the creative process, and that's why bringstorming includes sharing prototypes and simulations with others.

If you're developing a product and you've built a prototype, bring it to the bringstorm meeting, talk about it, pass it around, let other people in your bringstorm group use it, and take note of *how* they use it. If members of your group keep using your prototype's cardboard control arm as a carrying handle, you've discovered an idea-blind spot: your prototype may need a handle, or its control arm may need to be moved, or both.

If you're developing a process, the same idea of letting others experience it applies. To share a process in a bringstorm meeting, you could record a roleplay of your process, make a flow chart, or simulate the process during the meeting. If you have a different method of sharing a process, feel free to use it too. Again, be sure to observe and learn from your team's response.

If you want even better feedback, step outside of your group and share your idea with a stranger. Find someone you've never met before and free them from the worry of hurting your feelings by saying something like "My crazy Uncle Lou is making these in his garage, and I can't decide if it's a good idea or not. What do you think of it?" Raw feedback from people who don't know or care anything about your idea is usually the best. Allowing these types of users to test your ideas is important because they will give you sugar-free feedback. They'll be rough with your prototype, they'll use it "incorrectly," or they'll point out some glaring flaw in your process that you overlooked—they'll treat your ideas like they *will* be treated. It isn't personal; it's feedback.

The sooner you get that kind of feedback, the better, so don't be afraid to share even your first prototype or simulation. They're just ideas, after all.

Steve Madden, the shoe designer, is a good example of someone who has reaped the benefits of sharing prototypes with complete strangers. In his shoe store in New York, Steve and his crew design, prototype, and fabricate a new shoe style and then put it on the shelf. If the new shoe sells, they make a few more pairs, and if those sell—boom, he knows he's got a hit on his hands (or feet). If it doesn't sell, then it's no big deal because he hasn't wasted a lot of time and money on a dud. Madden's confidence to share prototypes early helps him and his team find successful designs before investing a lot of effort, a method that helps drive his billion-dollar business.

The sooner you share your prototype with others, the sooner you'll understand what works and what doesn't. And learning your idea's strengths and weaknesses early will help you succeed sooner.

Get New Eyes

In addition to testing ideas, another way you can expose idea-blind-spots is to use a tool my sculpture professor called *new eyes*.

As a college sophomore in a sculpting class, I struggled to sculpt a bust of the French writer Voltaire. Despite my best effort and hours of struggle, my sculpture looked more like Homer Simpson. Wanting to end my struggle, I asked my professor for help. After looking over my work (and my frustration) he said, "you need new eyes." He told me to get away from the project for a while—go on a walk, go work on something else, go to the gym, go wherever—and then come back. Getting away from the project, he said, would give my frustrations time to evaporate and help me see my project through new eyes when I returned. And he was right.

After getting away, I came back, looked at my work, and was able to see what I needed to do to reshape it, to turn Homer Simpson into Voltaire.

Whenever you find yourself or your team in love with or frustrated by an idea during the testing stage (or any stage, for that matter), take some time away from it. Take time to shed your old eyes and then revisit the idea with new ones. If you do, you'll be able to spot and fix idea-blind-spots with ease.

Shed Your Ego

Testing prototypes and processes to discover idea-blind-spots not only improves your ideas, it helps you shed your ego too. As you test ideas, you'll learn to get comfortable with the notion that any creation you share is imperfect and subject to change. During my career, I never built the perfect prototype or process on my first attempt. Creating or improving anything is an iterative endeavor. It requires a *'til- it's-right attitude*, meaning you have to shed your ego and break your emotional attachment to your ideas. The old Burger King slogan "have it your way" doesn't apply here. Your way may not be (and likely isn't) the best or even the only way. So if you discover an idea-blind-spot or if some new input requires you to rebuild your prototype or change your simulation for the umpteenth time, do it. It's just part of the process. It will be worth it.

Yes, shed egos and share ideas! Let's do this together. Let's close our eyes, breathe in deeply through the nose, exhale slowly through the mouth, and let our egos fall away—ah...that's better. With our egos gone, we're prepared to share prototypes, accept feedback, and improve ideas.

Chapter Summary

- Test ideas to reveal idea-blind-spots.
- Test ideas at the "research-quality" development level, and test early before investing in presentation-level idea development.
- Ideas are meant to be shared—especially with people who don't know about or care about your idea.
- Periodically take breaks from the project so you can see it through "new eyes" when you return to it.
- Shed your ego, test and share your ideas, accept feedback, and make improvements.

4

Ideation Pages, Bringstorm Pages, Keepers, and Losers

"He who is best prepared can best serve his moment of inspiration." — Samuel T. Coleridge

Have you ever been in the Rocky Mountains during a summer thunderstorm? It's unforgettable, especially when you experience a storm the way I did: at scout camp, at night, underprepared, and in a flimsy-indoor-certified tent (a kids play tent). I don't remember if it was the thunder, the wind, or the drops of water splashing on my face that woke a twelve-year-old me up during that night's storm, but I do remember the tent's thin walls whipping and dripping, my tent buddy, Greg, shaking his head at me in disappointment, and both of us not sleeping another wink. In retrospect, I have no idea why I thought that crappy little tent would be able to withstand the harsh realities of high-alpine camping, but for some reason I did.

These days, I can't help but wonder why many of us still cling to the belief that we can show up to a meeting unprepared and magically pull revolutionary ideas or solutions out of thin air. Sure, occasionally a revolutionary idea or the perfect solution hits us like a bolt of lightning, but I submit that *most* of those flashes of inspiration come after a fair amount of preparation.

In bringstorming, preparation is the foundation of inspiration. The last few chapters show how to prepare for a bringstorm meeting by defining the project's purpose, exploring alone, and testing your ideas as needed. In this chapter, I'll show the difference between ideation and bringstorm pages and how to use them.

Ideation Pages

As explained in previous chapters, to prepare effectively, you need to spend time on your own exploring, generating, and prototyping ideas and recording them on ideation pages. Ideation pages are records of your creative journey that contain lots of ideas that are supported by sketches, notes, web-addresses, internet video links, etc. And here's the thing: ideation pages can be private. You don't have to share them with anyone. So don't fret about spelling, grammar, penmanship, or your ability to draw. As long as *you* can read and understand what's on your ideation pages, that's good enough. And while these rough records of ideas are usually intended to be viewed and reviewed by one person (you), you, of course, can share them if you want to get early feedback on your ideas. It's your choice.

Here are two ideation pages I made while exploring ideas for a grasshopper exhibit. Remember though, I'm a product designer and an art director, so my ideation pages may look very different from yours. And that's okay.

Josh Farnworth

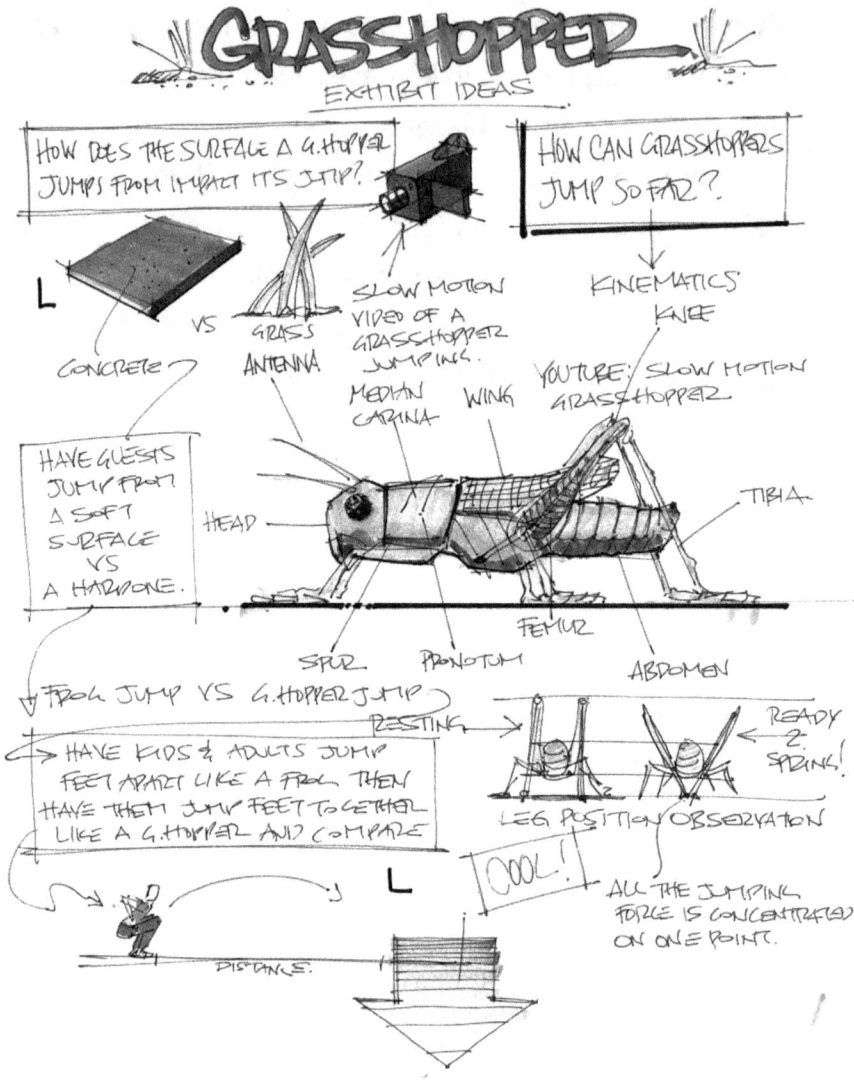

Bringstorm

Ideation pages like these are rough and eclectic records of your creative journey as you explore different ideas that connect to your purpose. They can contain multiple solutions to the problem you're trying to solve, links to sources, clippings from magazines, etc.

Keepers and Losers

Part of the process of preparing to share includes evaluating and categorizing your ideas. After you have spent time exploring, generating, and recording ideas on ideation pages, you'll need to take a moment to review and categorize every idea you've come up with. After you're done exploring, review your ideation pages and separate your ideas into one of two categories: keepers and losers. *Keepers* are strong ideas that clearly connect to the project's purpose (the ideas you'll potentially share during a bringstorm meeting). And *losers* are weak ideas that you can abandon. The way I categorize my ideas is simple. As I review my ideation pages, I write a capital letter "K" next to the ideas that are keepers and a capital letter "L" next to ideas that are losers. Then, out of the ideas that are keepers, I choose one, two, or three ideas (the best of the keepers) to turn into bringstorm pages.

Bringstorm Pages

Unlike ideation pages that are usually private and can contains lots of ideas, bringstorm pages are meant to be shared with your bringstorm team, and each page focuses on clearly demonstrating only one idea.

Because bringstorm pages are made to communicate individual ideas to other members of your team, they require more structure than ideation pages. Every bringstorm page should contain the following: a title with at least two-bracketed keywords beneath it; a short, written description of the idea; and any appropriate supporting material that was developed or discovered while exploring alone (sketches, notes, images, web addresses, video links, pictures of prototypes, etc.) See the example below.

JOSH FARNWORTH

Tympanum Headphones (insect, grasshopper)

Grasshoppers don't have ears like humans. Grasshoppers hear through an organ called a tympanum. A tympanum is a membrane stretched across a frame that is backed by air sacks and sensory neurons.

This idea is designed to give museum guests the experience of hearing like a grasshopper.

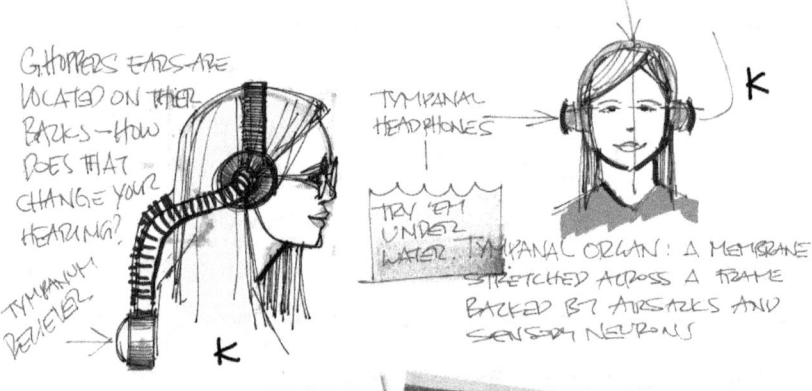

Tympanum (I think)

BRINGSTORM

Tympanum Headphones Prototype

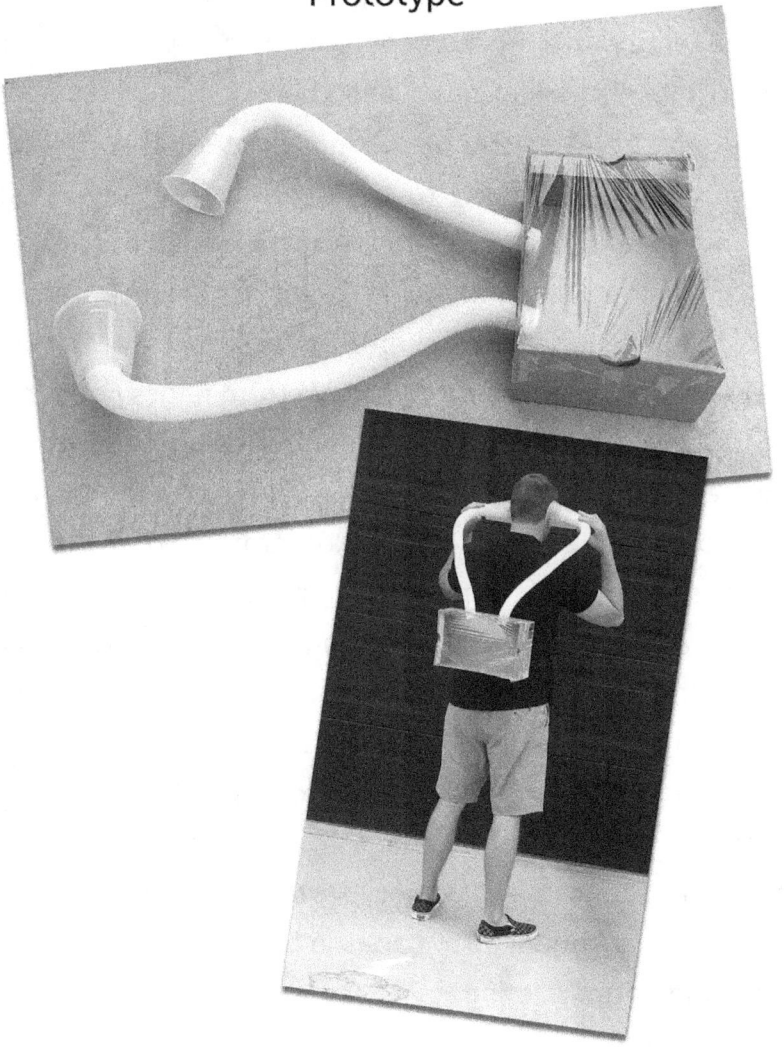

Bringstorm pages clearly demonstrate and support a single idea that connects with your project's purpose; they are meant to be shared with team members during a bringstorm meeting to facilitate discussion and collaboration.

In addition to communicating a potential solution to the problem you're out to solve, bringstorm pages also serve a second purpose: they record ideas so they can be stored inside the bringstorm library for future reference and use (see Chapter Seven). Because they are stored inside the bringstorm library, bringstorm pages need to be searchable, which is why, as I mentioned a few sentences ago, every bringstorm page needs at least two bracketed keywords beneath its title. Remember to make one of those keywords general and the other more specific (see grasshopper bringstorm page). Doing so will make searching for and finding ideas inside the bringstorm library much easier.

After you've completed this process, print off enough copies of your bringstorm pages for each member of your group and round up any prototypes that support them. With your prepared bringstorm pages in hand, you are ready for the bringstorm meeting.

■ ■ ■

To illustrate the larger process of preparing for a bringstorm meeting, from defining your project's purpose to creating bringstorm pages, here's a real-life example.

A few years ago, a small creative team I was on was given the assignment to re-imagine an unpopular exhibit space inside a children's museum. The museum's head mucky-mucks had little interest in how we changed it—they just wanted the space and its exhibits to attract and engage guests while jiving with the museum's theme: "A City for Kids."

With these requirements in mind, my team and I held a quick meeting. In the meeting we discussed the project and then created a purpose statement that went something like this: "Because we want to strengthen and educate families and individuals, we are going to create an exhibit space that inspires people of all ages to learn and grow together within the museum's 'A City for Kids' theme." After discussing and defining our purpose, we agreed to spend a few hours during the week exploring, generating, prototyping, and recording ideas alone. We scheduled an end-of-the-week bringstorm meeting, and off we went.

As we spent time exploring alone during the week, each of us came up with lots of different ideas about how to change the space. Some of the ideas I came up with were a video game store about pixels, a funky furniture store about ergonomics, an air traffic control room about communication, an art gallery where kids could make and show off their art work, a print shop about the printing process, and a rock-climbing gym. At the end of the week, I reviewed and evaluated my ideas, categorized each one as a keeper or loser, selected the two best ideas from my keeper's category (the video game and funky furniture stores), and made a bringstorm page for each one.

With my bringstorm pages finished, I made copies of them to hand out, rounded up any prototypes I'd built, and kicked my feet up on my desk for a few minutes, confident that I was ready for the bringstorm meeting.

How Much Preparation is Enough?

The world-famous graphic designer Milton Glaser helps me decide if I've done enough with his statement that "just enough is more." In the context of sharing ideas, this means you don't over prepare or under prepare; just make each idea you bring easy to communicate and easy to understand, give it a bit of credibility with some supporting content (sketches, notes, web addresses, video links, prototypes, etc.), and get on with the process. Laboring over and fine-tuning ideas that have a high probability of not making it past a bringstorm meeting is, like polishing the silverware on the Hindenburg, pointless. So don't get caught up in bringing the perfect idea to a bringstorm meeting, instead, bring a couple of great ideas that are anchored to the project's purpose and that are imperfectly but clearly represented on bringstorm pages, and let the perfect idea grow from those.

With that said, I think I've given you just enough information about how to get ready for a bringstorm meeting, so let's get on with it.

Chapter Summary

- Preparation is the foundation of inspiration.
- To prepare for a bringstorm meeting, (1) define the project's purpose; (2) explore and prototype alone while recording your ideas on ideation pages; and (3) pick one, two, or three of your best ideas, and make a bringstorm page for each.
- Choose a single format for your team's bringstorm pages that includes a title, keywords, and rough-but-clear descriptions and depictions of ideas.

5

The Bringstorm Meeting

"Luck is a matter of preparation meeting opportunity." — Lucius Annaeus Seneca

After all your preparation, you're finally ready to present your ideas in a bringstorm meeting. Bringstorm meetings boost creativity, expose idea-blind-spots, and deliver purpose-fulfilling ideas. They are meant to be simple, informal, and adaptable: if you and your team can dedicate two hours to a project, take thirty-seven minutes to explore alone, eleven minutes to evaluate and categorize your ideas, twelve minutes to put together a few bringstorm pages, and spend the last hour sharing your ideas and collaborating in a bringstorm meeting.

So what does a bringstorm meeting look like? Simply bring, share, collaborate, review, and vote. That's all there is to a bringstorm meeting. This chapter will walk you through these steps. As always, it's a good idea to tailor the principles I share to fit you and your team's needs.

Bring

Before I share how to hold a bringstorm meeting, I think it's important to share what each team member needs to bring. At the beginning of every bringstorm meeting, everyone that's participating is required to have the following:

- a pencil or pen for ranking ideas and taking notes;
- copies of his or her top one, two, or three ideas outlined in bringstorm pages to give to each member of the team;
- relevant prototypes;
- a silenced cell phone for making videos if needed; and
- a teachable and open attitude.

A few other items that can help facilitate a successful bringstorm meeting but are not required are a laptop or tablet, a projector, a white board, and a small table for displaying prototypes. Having healthy snacks, water, and treats available is usually a good idea, too.

Share

Every team member needs to share at least one idea during a bringstorm meeting. But how to share is almost as important as what to share. Have you ever attended a presentation, speech, or lecture and found your ability to understand it hampered by the speaker's highfalutin' prose, arrogant tone, industry-specific jargon, or confusing sentence structure? Heaven knows I have, and it's not an enjoyable experience. To make bringstorm meetings enjoyable and effective, make the ideas you share easy for everyone on your team to understand. Whenever possible, make your ideas so simple to understand that your teammates could finish sharing them if you were brained with a croquet mallet half way through your presentation.

To make your ideas easy for others to understand, here's a few things you can do:

- Stick to the big picture. Going into too much detail about an idea often causes others to become confused or lose interest.
- Use everyday language. Using common words to describe your ideas makes them easy for everyone to understand. Using flowery language and obscure words does the opposite.

- Give yourself a short amount of time to share an idea. Limiting the time you have to share an idea to a few minutes will help you share only the most important parts of the idea.
- Share your idea with someone not involved in the project and see if they "get it." If they don't, you know you need to make your idea easier to understand.
- Don't use two when one will do. Using too many charts, graphs, images, videos, or prototypes to support your ideas will make them more complicated than they need to be.

Collaborate

As each idea is shared, take time to explore it as a group. Talk about its strengths and weaknesses; ask questions about it; test its prototypes; develop it further using random word associations, a quick brainstorm, a mind map, the internet, roleplay, and/or any other creative thinking tool not listed. Truly collaborate about each idea. And as you collaborate, if a good idea sparks a better one, you're free to explore that idea too.

Review

After everyone has shared their ideas and collaborated, have whoever is leading the meeting quickly review each idea that was presented with the rest of the group. This step is meant to be quick, so if you're leading the meeting, don't spend a lot of time thoroughly reviewing each idea. Instead, I suggest reading the title of each idea's bringstorm page, sharing a few important details about each idea after reading its title, and then moving on to the next step: voting.

Vote

At the end of every bringstorm meeting, everyone involved gets to vote for the idea that they feel best fulfills the project's purpose. The voting process is simple: after team members have shared their ideas, have whoever is leading the meeting lead the vote; that person lists the title of each idea that was shared and displays the list to the voters; everyone votes via hand raising or secret ballot (you decide which method works best for your team); the leader tallies up the votes, and the idea with the most votes wins!

Sample Bringstorm Meeting Agenda

To summarize the bring, share, collaborate, review, and vote process, here's a handy-dandy outline of a typical agenda you could use to run your own bringstorm meeting:

1. If you haven't already, pick someone to lead the meeting. Welcome everyone. Grab and eat snacks.
2. *Bring:* make sure everyone has come prepared with what they need.
3. *Share:* Pass out bringstorm pages and have team members present their ideas.
4. *Collaborate:* Collaborate by refining, developing, and evaluating each idea with the group as it is shared.
5. *Review:* After everyone has shared their ideas, thank everyone for their work and, as a group, rapidly review each one.
6. *Vote:* Out the pool of ideas, choose a winner via a vote.

Winners, Keepers, and Losers

In the world of bringstorming, ideas are assigned to one of three categories: winners, keepers, or losers. In Chapter Four, you learned about two of these categories: keepers and losers. Keepers are the strong ideas that connect with the project's purpose, and losers are the weak ideas that don't. Of the keepers, some will rise above to be categorized as winners.

Winning ideas, or "winners," have three components: (1) they are the strongest ideas that directly connect to the project's purpose, (2) they are the ideas that receive the most votes after a bringstorm meeting, and (3) they are chosen out of the pool of keepers that are brought to a bringstorm meeting (no losers allowed at the meeting). Now, you might be asking, "Shouldn't the title of the category be singular instead of plural? Shouldn't it be titled *winner* instead of *winners*?" While the goal of every bringstorm meeting is to find one winning idea, the meetings often produce multiple winning ideas; therefore, it's called the "winners" category. In Chapter Six, I'll share more about what to do when a bringstorm produces multiple winners, but for now, let's talk about what happens to winners and keepers after a bringstorm meeting.

Because every idea that is brought to a bringstorm is a keeper, it remains in that category unless it is chosen to be a winner. If an idea remains a keeper because it is not chosen as a winner, save it in the "Keepers" folder inside the bringstorm library for future reference and use (see Chapter Seven). If an idea is chosen to be a winner, add it to the winners category by saving it in the "Winners" folder inside the bringstorm library. Then go on to developing the winning idea(s).

A Bringstorm Meeting Example from Real Life

As straightforward as a bringstorm meeting is, a concrete example is always helpful.

Continuing with the children's museum example from Chapter Four, an hour or so after I'd finished preparing and making copies of my bringstorm pages, I picked them up, grabbed the prototypes I'd made, and headed to the museum's fabrication shop for the bringstorm meeting. Inside the shop, the members of my team (Dean, Gina, Cici, Mitch) and I arranged some chairs near a wheeled white board, a folding table, and a dusty PC. With the space arranged, I welcomed everyone, reviewed the project's purpose, and asked Gina to share her ideas first.

Taking her place at the front of the group, Gina shared her first idea: a detective agency with wall-sized search-and-find exhibits. Along with her idea, she also shared a search-and-find prototype she'd made, which was a five-inch by two-foot, clear, plastic tube filled with a variety of knick knacks and toys that you could visually search through to find a specific item. After introducing us to the idea and sharing her prototype, Gina gave us a little more insight into the idea and how she thought it would work in the children's museum, and boom! The collaboration was on.

With a solid understanding of Gina's idea, the team (Gina included) spoke freely about it—we brainstormed about it, added to it, subtracted from it, asked questions; shared our perspective, excitement, and concerns; sketched and wrote on the white board; and tried out the prototype—we truly collaborated. And a short time later, we were confident we had a solid option on our hands, an option that connected to the project's purpose and fit the museum's "City for Kids" theme.

And so the bringstorm meeting went. As each team member shared the ideas and prototypes they'd brought, we collaborated about each one, about ideas like a video game store with exhibits about pixels, a playground with equipment that taught kids about balance, an auto shop where kids could perform basic maintenance tasks on a kid-size-plastic car, and a radio station that broadcast to radios inside the museum to name a few. Out of the ideas that were shared, some of them tied directly to the project's purpose, inspired excitement within the team, and were potential winners. And others weren't.

After we had listened to and collaborated about each idea, I thanked everyone for their work, quickly reviewed the ideas that were shared and listed them on the white board, and then we voted. After the vote, the auto-shop idea was the clear winner. Confident that our winning auto-shop idea fulfilled our purpose, we set a date for a second bringstorm meeting to share ideas about the different exhibits that would fill the new space.

Chapter Summary

- Keep presentations simple.
- Bring only ideas that are "keepers" to bringstorm meetings.
- Bring, share, collaborate, review, and vote. Winning ideas are the best ideas that connect to the project's purpose.

6

Strategies, Insights, and Advice

"It's not personal; it's feedback." — Me

The bringstorm process isn't complicated, but I've facilitated enough bringstorm sessions/meetings to have experienced a few of the common challenges that can occur when bringstorming. I also have ideas for how to handle these scenarios that may help you if and when you run into similar situations.

What to Do When You Have More Than One Winning Idea

In Chapter Five, I mentioned that bringstorm meetings often produce multiple winning ideas. When that happens, how do you choose between them? Depending on how much time you have, I suggest doing one of the following:

- If you have plenty of time, take the winning ideas, run them through the entire bringstorm process a second time, and pick a winner.
- If time is scarce, take them through a condensed version of the bringstorm process. Give each team member an hour-or-so to further explore and evaluate the winning ideas alone, hold a second bringstorm meeting, and pick a winner.
- If you're completely out of time, pick one of the winning ideas and run with it. Remember that indecision reduces momentum. So just pick a great idea out of the bunch and move forward with confidence. Doing so will keep your project moving at the right pace.

An additional thing you can do to break a stalemate between ideas is to pay attention to who voted for what. As we all know, teams are made up of individuals, and individuals have their strengths and weaknesses, subjects in which they are experts and subjects in which they are less competent. I bring this up because as you and your team vote on ideas, you might notice that relative to each idea, the value of each team member's vote fluctuates. For example, if you're bringstorming ideas about *improving the structural integrity of passenger jet wings*, an accountant's vote is less valuable than an engineer's vote. And on the flip side, if you're bringstorming ideas about how to structure a jet company's accounts payable, the accountant's vote is more valuable. So an additional way to break a stalemate between ideas is to give the team member(s) with the most credibility an extra vote. But most of the time, being aware of your team members' strengths and weaknesses and voting accordingly works wonders.

How to Avoid Confrontation by Using Good Communication

While we can't control our team members' levels of relaxation or how they will react to the feedback we give them, we can be constructive and courteous. To help keep feedback direct without making it harsh, try these tips:

- *Remember the law of reciprocation.* The law of reciprocation says that when someone does something nice for you, you are inclined do something nice for them and vice versa. If you're genuinely engaged in exploring, evaluating, and riffing on Tom's ideas about logistics, then Tom, quite naturally, will be genuinely engaged in exploring, evaluating, and riffing on your ideas too. Conversely, if you are cynical, aloof, or chilly toward Tom's ideas, he'll probably return the favor. As such, during your upcoming bringstorms, remember to be engaged, genuine, and respectful: if a strong idea is shared, say so and explore it; if a weak idea is shared, explore it if you want, and if it leads to a dead end don't hesitate to say so. Just say it with sugar because we're all human, and we all have the tendency to treat our ideas as extensions of ourselves.

- *Avoid using personal pronouns.* When giving feedback, instead of saying, "your idea doesn't fit the project," try saying, "this idea doesn't fit the project." Avoiding personal pronouns will help take the teeth out of comments that bite.
- *Listen first and speak second.* In his book *The Seven Habits of Highly Effective People*, Stephen Covey encourages everyone to "seek first to understand . . . then to be understood." What he means is this: when we communicate with others, we need to "listen with the intent to understand" instead of listening with the "intent to reply." When we take the time to truly understand and appreciate a person's ideas, beliefs, or point of view, we create an environment that is cooperative instead of confrontational, an environment where great ideas and good vibes flourish.

How to Keep Calm and Bringstorm On

We're all human. We all tend to treat our ideas as extensions of ourselves. And we all have feelings, egos, political, and religious or moral beliefs that can get involved in our ideas and cause unnecessary waves that may capsize our creative process or drain the creative energy out of our group. For example, during a bringstorm meeting, Jim storms out of the office because his ideas didn't make the cut, or Thad suggests using wood to build a science exhibit, and because she loves the forest, Elizabeth launches into a verbal *save the trees* campaign, effectively killing the creative flow by cowing the team members with her personal preferences.

These examples seem silly, but I've seen these kinds of scenarios happen and had these defensive feelings myself, so I know it can and does happen to many of us. Here's some tips for how to stay professional, even when we're tempted to get a little over-protective of our ideas.

When an individual or the group rejects or accepts one or more of our ideas, we can feel like they are rejecting or accepting us too. In this scenario, it's tempting to experience strong emotions, either positive or negative. However, highly emotional responses can take you out of the professional zone quickly. To avoid getting too emotional, especially if your idea is getting rejected, try some of the following strategies:

1. *Uncouple yourself from your ideas*: Remember, this is not about you. It's about a concept. Keeping you and your ideas separated in your mind takes some practice, but here are two things you can do to uncouple yourself from your ideas. First, whenever an idea you've shared is criticized or rejected, remember that it's not personal; it's feedback—literally repeat this in your head a few times if you need to. And second, change your perspective. Feedback is actually an improving and refining force you can use to make your idea better. It's not tearing you or your idea apart.
2. *Practice tactical breathing:* This is a technique that is used by military personnel, first responders, and professional athletes to calm down in stressful situations. Here's how to do it: in your head, steadily count to four as you breath in, hold your breath and count to four again, and count to four a third time while exhaling. Do this three, four, or five times, and you should feel yourself relax.
3. *Release the moment*: Sometimes it's best to just let harsh comments or criticism go. Take the rapper

Jay-Z's advice and "go and brush your shoulders off." If someone offends you, make a conscious choice to let it go and move on.

Take the Bringstorm Oath

Winning ideas are often discovered after periods of struggle, and it's during these periods of time that being relaxed emotionally is most important. When an individual or team is struggling to find answers to difficult problems, feelings of rejection, frustration, and impatience are the easiest to lose control of. And it's during these stressful times that team members tend to get offended. If being relaxed is the one thing to do during a bringstorm meeting, getting offended is the one thing *not* to do.

Becoming offended is tempting because when we're offended, we excuse ourselves from listening or reasoning or participating or acting rationally, because, hey, we're offended. It's also tempting to be offended as a way to get others to appease us by softening their feedback or changing their votes. Why? Because they work with us, and who wants to work with a colleague that's upset with them? No one. But using the adult equivalent of a tantrum (by acting offended) to manipulate team members squelches your team's creative vibe and undermines its ability to discover winning ideas. And what is really more important to you, having your idea win, or having the best idea win? Your idea may be the best idea, but it may not be. So choose not to get offended, and, as evidence of your choice, right here and now, take the bringstorm oath:

> I do solemnly swear that during every bringstorm meeting my skin will become as thick as a rhinoceros,' that I will not take offense, and that I will use positive feedback to reinforce my personal belief that I am a genius and negative feedback to improve my ideas. And if I break my oath, I swear that as penance, I will allow my team to record me preforming an improvised dance to a song of their choice, and I will not restrict them from posting their recordings on a social media platform of their choosing. So help me Zeus!

The Scale of Enthusiasm

Because bringstorming involves sharing and exploring many different ideas, it can be difficult to remember which ideas you want to vote for and which ones you don't. To remedy this, I'll introduce you to a simple tool I call the Scale of Enthusiasm.

The Scale of Enthusiasm allows team members to rate

ideas on a scale from one to ten with an important caveat: you can't rate any idea a seven. Only the numbers one, two, three, four, five, six, eight, nine, and ten are game. Credit for this caveat goes to the CEO (name withheld) who told Kyle Maynard who told Tim Ferriss who shared it on his podcast (episode 284). The reason for eliminating the number seven is this: rating something a seven is a copout—nobody really likes an idea that's a seven. If an idea is worthy of an eight, nine, or ten, you know that you like, really like, or love it. If you rate an idea a six or lower you know it needs work or it's not up to snuff. So as your teammates present their ideas, pay attention to the level of enthusiasm each idea brings. If an idea is shared and it sparks your imagination and ignites a collaborative fire within your team, write a ten in the corner of its bringstorm page. If you hear crickets, write a one. If the response is mediocre, give it a four or a five or a six or a two-point-one-seven-four—you get the picture. Writing your level of enthusiasm on each idea's bringstorm page makes it easy to remember which ideas you want to vote for, so don't forget to do it.

. . .

In summary, as ideas are shared, rate them. At the end of a bringstorm meeting, give everyone a few minutes to review the ideas and Scale of Enthusiasm ratings, and then vote. If there is a clear winner, go with it, or, if you feel the need, have the team explore the winning idea further by focusing an additional bringstorm around it. If at the end of a bringstorm meeting, there are multiple winners, focus an additional bringstorm around them, and then vote for a winner. And finally, if you have multiple ideas that are winners and you're out of time, don't procrastinate choosing one. Pick one of the winning ideas, save the other(s) inside the bringstorm library, and move forward with the project.

Like learning to play the piano, landing a round-off-backhand spring, or driving a stick shift, your bringstorming skills will improve as you use them. Over time and with practice, each member of your team will become less self-conscious, care less about whose idea is picked, and care more about each project being a success. Over time, you and your team will relax and mesh and find your stride, fine-tuning and tailoring the process as you go. Soon bringstorming will be second nature, like walking or eating.

Chapter Summary

- When you have more than one winning idea, keep the project's momentum by choosing one idea to pursue with confidence.

- Remember the Law of Reciprocation. Actively and respectfully participate in bringstorm meetings.
- Uncouple yourself from your ideas, remember the bringstorm oath, and practice letting go if you start feeling defensive.
- Don't use personal pronouns when giving feedback.
- Use the Scale of Enthusiasm to rate ideas as they are shared.

7

The Bringstorm Library

"A library is the delivery room for the birth of ideas, a place where history comes to life."
—Norman Cousins

Libraries are like elephants: they never forget. When I was a kid, back in the eighties, my mom worked at the Orem Public Library. I spent countless hours wandering between its towering bookshelves, perusing books and periodicals, napping here and there, clambering up and down the stairs, riding the elevator, and following my mom around as she helped patrons. As I followed her, I remember being impressed by how organized the library was, how a patron could ask my mom where a book was located, and after a few moments of searching through a large card file, she could tell them where to find it or lead them right to it.

Libraries work well because they are well organized and

because they help us learn from and remember good ideas. Your bringstorm library shouldn't be any different. In this chapter, I'll share what a bringstorm library is and how to keep it organized so that you and your team will never forget the good ideas you've worked to bringstorm.

What is a Bringstorm Library?

A bringstorm library is a collection of the bringstorm pages that are brought to bringstorm meetings—the *keepers* and the *winners*. It's a digital catalog that team members can explore, research, use to jog memory, and suppress loss aversion. It can also save your bacon when you need a great idea in a pinch.

How is the Bringstorm Library Organized?

Organizing the bringstorm library is simple: inside whatever platform you choose (Google Docs, Dropbox, Windows, Mac OS X) make a folder titled "Bringstorm Library." Inside the Bringstorm Library folder, make two more folders. Title one folder *Winners* and the other *Keepers*. After each bringstorm, save the winning bringstorm page inside the *Winners* folder and save the bringstorm pages that are selected as keepers inside the *Keepers* folder. And that's it.

Now you might be thinking that after hundreds or even thousands of bringstorm pages are saved inside the bringstorm library that it will be impossible to find what you're looking for. Not true. Because every bringstorm page must be saved using **its title and keywords** (see Chapter Four), you'll be able to open the bringstorm library folder, type keywords into your platform's search tool, and find what you're looking for. Just like we type keywords into online search engines to find content on the internet, you'll use your platform's search tool to find ideas inside the bringstorm library.

How to Save Prototypes in the Bringstorm Library

Building prototypes to test and add credibility to ideas is a crucial part of the creative process; however, because physical objects take up physical space, storing tangible prototypes in the bringstorm library can be problematic. To help you solve this problem, I suggest saving them inside the bringstorm library. After a prototype has served its purpose, take pictures of it, record a video of it in action (if necessary), add the pictures and video to the idea's bringstorm page, and then resave that page inside the library. The same idea applies to intangible prototypes or other types of tests too. Be sure to save them along with their bringstorm pages.

Taking pictures and recording videos of prototypes

(making them digital), attaching them to the appropriate bringstorm page, and resaving them inside the bringstorm library not only frees up precious shelf space, but doing so also makes finding and reviewing past prototypes easy. So do it.

Why the Bringstorm Library Should be Digital

The reasons for making your bringstorm library digital should be obvious, but I'll share a few reasons anyway. Making your library digital makes it accessible from almost anywhere, it eliminates the hassle of storing a growing hodgepodge of sketch papers and notes and pictures and videos and prototypes, it makes it easy to find and explore past bringstorm pages, it enhances collaboration, and on and on. With a few of the many benefits of using a digital library in mind, let me make one suggestion: all bringstorm pages added to the bringstorm library need to be saved in a widely-used, single format like a PDF (one format to rule them all). In the long run, doing so will make using the bringstorm library more efficient and more enjoyable to use—trust me. . . or don't and suffer the consequences, mwaa haaa haaa!

The Bringstorm Librarian

Melodrama aside, every library needs a librarian to keep things organized and the bringstorm library is no different. To keep it organized, the librarian does four things:

1. Acts as a gate keeper. All bringstorm pages enter the library through the librarian.
2. Saves bringstorm pages inside the appropriate folders.
3. Follows up with team members about submitting their bringstorm pages.
4. Makes sure that every bringstorm page submitted has the following:

    a. a title with at least two keywords attached,
    b. a short description of the idea, and
    c. supporting material that helps communicate the idea such as sketches, notes, images, videos, pictures of prototypes, etc.

And that's it. The librarian's job is *not* to be the rest of the team's secretary. Each member of a bringstorm team is responsible for

- making sure the pages he or she submits meet the previously mentioned requirements,
- saving pages in the predetermined format, and
- sending those pages to the librarian.

If a team member fails to fulfill these responsibilities, we'll chalk it up to the creative world's version of natural selection. Bringstorm pages that don't adapt to the predetermined format and/or don't make it to the librarian, don't survive, with one exception: the winning idea must make it into the library.

Before we move on, here's a hint about the bringstorm librarian's role: make it a temporary one. Try not to make one team member the eternal bringstorm librarian. Switch it up regularly. Share the load.

Accessibility

All bringstorm pages need to be accessible to everyone on the team; each team member should have access to the bringstorm library and be free to use and peruse the ideas that are in it. As I mentioned earlier, operating systems like Windows and Mac OS X are great platforms to use for your bringstorm library as long as everyone can access it via the internet, but Google Docs and Dropbox are great options too. Whichever one you pick, make sure it's easy to access and available to each member of your team. 'Nough said.

Chapter Summary

- Organize the bringstorm library with a digital file system accessible to every team member.
- Include a title that includes at least two keywords, a short description of the idea, and material that supports the idea on every bringstorm page.
- Take the time to digitize bringstorm pages and prototypes to save in the library. Unsaved ideas will be forgotten.
- Share the load. The bringstorm librarian isn't the team's secretary.

8

Repeat the Process

"Murder your darlings." — Sir Arthur Quiller-Couch.

In any endeavor, the first attempt rarely ends in success. Two years ago, I went to a local mixed-martial-arts gym and signed up to learn Brazilian Jiu-Jitsu, a combat sport that focuses on grappling and ground fighting. As you may have guessed, when I experienced my first round of Jiu-Jitsu, I got owned. About ninety seconds after the round started, I found my head, neck, and arm securely locked in a triangle choke. The rest of the class didn't go much better. At the end of the class, I approached the instructor and talked with him about my losing streak. As we spoke, he shared a quote with me from the grand master of Brazilian-Jiu-Jitsu, Carlos Gracie Jr.: "In Jiu-Jitsu, you either win or you learn."

The same principle applies to bringstorming, problem solving, and idea generation: you either find the solution to the problem, the winning idea, or you learn. So, if your first bringstorm process doesn't yield the ideal result, further explore the *keeper* ideas that came from it, or give it another whirl. You'll have learned more this time, and sooner than you think, the idea you've been searching for will appear.

How many times do you need to repeat the process before you find a winning idea? As many times as it takes. Sometimes winning ideas appear almost instantly, like light when a bulb is switched on. But most often, winning ideas take time to discover; they appear gradually, like light at sunrise. If the winning idea doesn't manifest itself within seconds, minutes, hours, or days, give it more time. Keep working and be patient. At some point, the failed attempts, the time spent exploring, and the consistent work will pay off.

Now, I realize this sounds a bit like hippie talk— "be patient maaaaan; peace, love, and ideas are like a sunrise, maaaaan." So to reconnect it with reality, I'll add this: no two bringstorm journeys are the same. Every time you go through the bringstorm process, you will discover new ideas. Because of this, you can be confident that repeating the bringstorm process won't be a waste of time; you'll always produce new and different results. You'll keep getting better at the process, and you'll keep getting better results.

Creativity Ain't Easy

Many people believe that being creative is relatively easy, mostly fun, and requires little work. The reason for this, in my opinion, is because they have the Hollywood version of creativity in their heads— after a short montage, a wild-eyed, intelligent, attractive, scientist creates a new whiz-bang-invention that saves a dude or damsel in distress. Or a young, pasty, bespectacled computer programmer has a flash of inspiration that saves earth from an alien attack. While these depictions of creative genius are obviously disconnected from reality, lots of people unintentionally embrace the idea that creativity "just comes" instead of facing the fact that creativity is actually hard work. It's ninety percent frustration, seven percent exhilaration, and three percent electricity.

Because many people, usually bosses, managers, or clients, think that being creative is generally easy and fun, you'll often encounter impatience with the creative process, especially when you have to repeat it. Which, if you think about it, is unreasonable and a bit humorous. I know whenever a boss, manager, or client is being impatient with me during the creative process, I often find myself chuckling on the inside because what they are really doing is asking, "Why haven't you already invented that thing that doesn't exist yet?" Aside from laughing to yourself in this situation, here are a few ways to deal with impatience, either your own or your client's:

- Create realistic timelines that give you and your team enough time to do the job correctly. In my experience, projects generally take far more time to finish than we expect—team members get sick, delivery trucks break down, computers glitch, clients requests changes midstream, and so on. To create realistic timelines without being able to predict the future, here's what I suggest:

    1. Break each project into stages, stages such as *research*, *development*, *production*, and *delivery*.
    b. Estimate the time it will take to complete each stage, adding a reasonable amount of "buffer time" to each estimate.
    3. Add up the estimates for each stage to get the total time for the project.
    4. Create a timeline that includes each stage of the project, and share your estimates and timeline with the rest of your team.
    5. If your team is confident that the estimates and timeline are realistic, get to work. If the team's not comfortable with the timeline, adjust it.

- Set clear expectations by describing each stage of a project to everyone involved and discuss what is going to be delivered at the end of each stage.
- Communicate progress regularly. Keep bosses, managers, and clients involved in the project by consistently reporting and discussing setbacks and leaps forward. This will also help you see the progress you're making more clearly and know what steps you need to take next.

∎ ∎ ∎

Creating or improving anything is hard because it often requires us to make multiple attempts, endure frustration, and deal with people who don't understand the process. But creative problem solving is also one of the most rewarding things you can do. Few things make you feel as good as finding a solution or making a product that improves the lives of others. And that's what bringstorming is all about.

Chapter Summary

- First attempts rarely end in success. Don't give up.
- You either win or you learn.
- Creating solutions takes as long as it takes.
- Don't be afraid to trash your trash and start over.
- To avoid frustration, plan and communicate.

9

A Helpful Hint

"Don't take forever to say something; you don't have that kind of time."— Me

This is a short book, and it's short for a reason. A few years back, I took an enlightening and attitude-correcting class on public speaking. One of the most helpful things I learned about public speaking was this: end a few minutes early—never go overtime. No matter how intriguing, compelling, or moving you think your speech is, your audience will be grateful to you for ending two or three minutes early and giving them back a little bit of their own time.

From the beginning, this book was meant to be short, simple, and accessible—easily read in an hour or so. So out of respect for your time, I'll give you a last kernel of wisdom, and then I'll put a cork in it.

I stumbled upon this kernel of wisdom one evening while

I was watching the comedian Dimitri Martin. Dimitri likes to use simple drawings during his comedy sets, and in the one I was watching he drew graphics like these about success:

Success — what people think it looks like (an upward diagonal arrow)

Success — what it really looks like (a tangled scribble ending in an upward arrow)

For some reason—I don't know why—people believe that the path to success is an inclined straight line. Well, Dimitri is right: it isn't. Truthfully, the path to success has more in common with a bowl of ramen noodles, full of loops, overlaps, and switchbacks. And the path to making successful products and processes isn't any different: it's unpredictable and winding, too. Because of this, it's easy to slip into a negative frame of mind when a project gets rough and team members become discouraged and fearful. To avoid discouragement and stay positive when the project inevitably experiences turbulence, try doing the following:

- Focus on how your work will benefit others.
- Visualize the day you deliver your stellar product or process.
- Remember that setbacks are a normal part of the process, and trust that you and your team have the tenacity and brains needed to overcome these challenges.
- Improv dance to an upbeat song of your choice ("You Make My Dreams" by Hall & Oates is an excellent option).

Regardless of the song you choose and how difficult a project is remember to press forward with faith in the process, faith in your team, and faith in yourself. If you do, you'll be rewarded. And look on the bright side: with bringstorming, you've got a new tool to add to your box of tricks, a tool that will help you complete future creative journeys with pizazz.

Happy bringstorming!

Chapter Summary

- End a little early.
- Expect the path to success to be messy.
- Improv dance when needed.

Appendix

Resources and Examples

For your reference, here is a summary of the steps of bringstorming to help jog your memory, complete with examples of my exploration process, sample ideation and bringstorm pages, and an example prototype.

Here are the steps of the bringstorm process:

1. **Define your purpose:** Define why you're doing the project and what it is you want to accomplish, what problem you are going to solve.
2. **Explore alone**: Spend some time exploring, discovering, creating, and prototyping solutions to the problem on your own and recording your thoughts and ideas on ideation pages as you go.
3. **Test**: Make simple, function-focused prototypes, and, if possible, test them with an audience.

4. **Prepare to share**: Take the time to make the ideas you've collected, created, and prototyped easy to communicate by organizing them into simple bringstorm pages.
5. **Hold a bringstorm meeting and vote**: Regroup with the members of your team, and take turns sharing and discussing the ideas that everyone brings. Vote on a winning idea.
6. **Keep a record**: Save the keepers and the winners in the bringstorm library.
7. **Repeat the process:** If the first bringstorm process didn't yield a winner or you want to further explore the winning idea you've picked, repeat the process—bringstorm as many times as you need to.

The images below are two ideation pages and a bringstorm page that I made while exploring ideas for diaper bags.

Ideation page examples

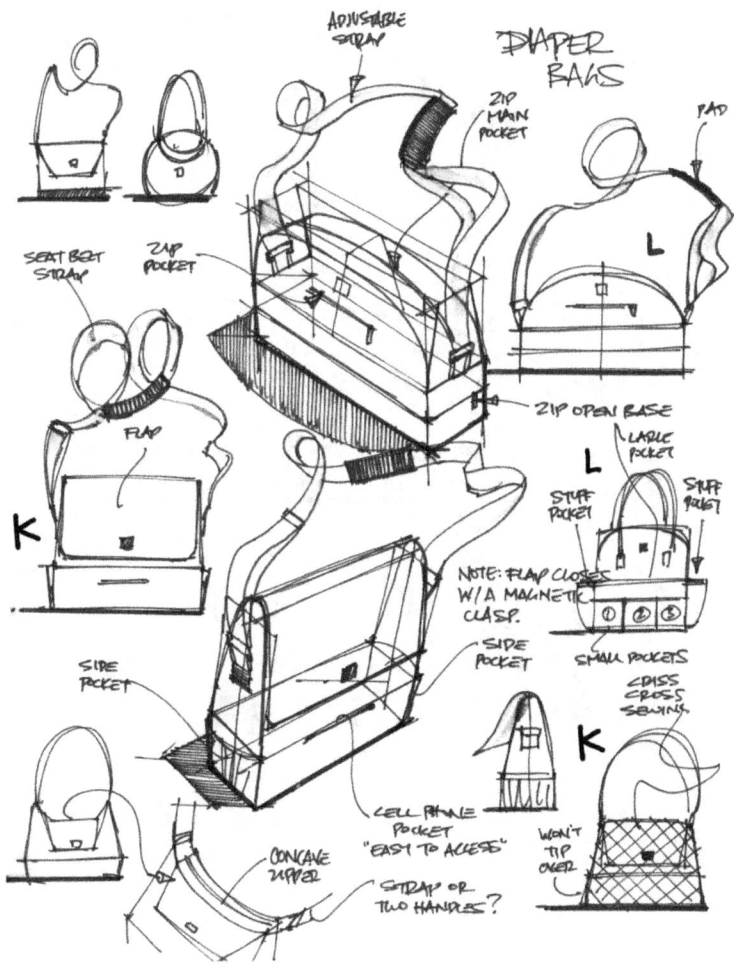

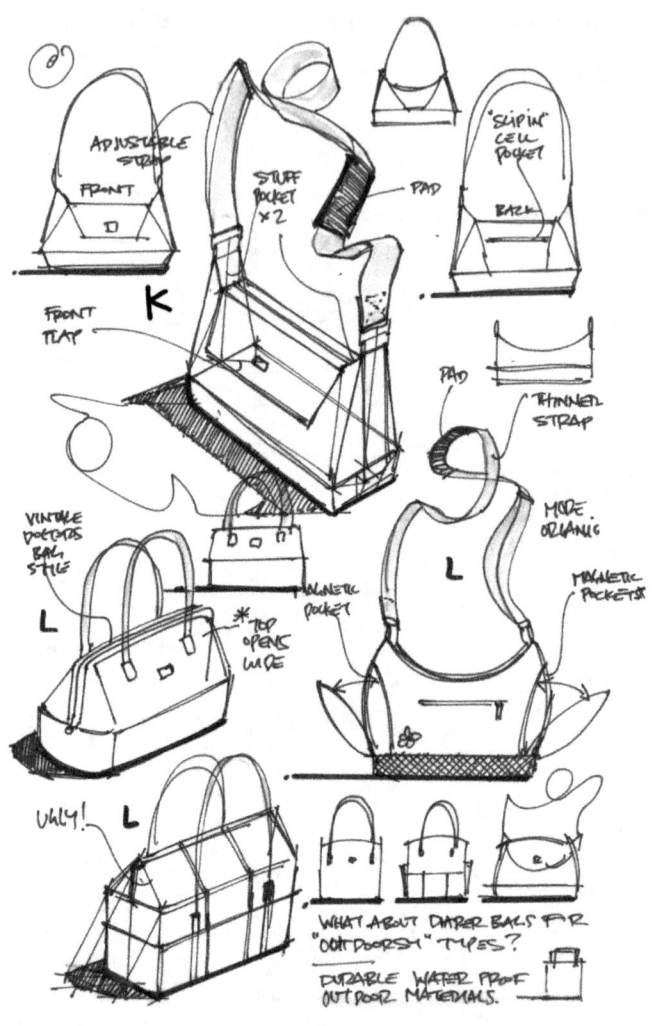

Bringstorm page example

Josh's Diaper Bag Concept
(diaper bag, simple, five pockets)

Many of today's diaper bags suffer from "feature creep." They contain useless features that don't make parents lives easier.

This idea is a simplified diaper bag with five pockets.

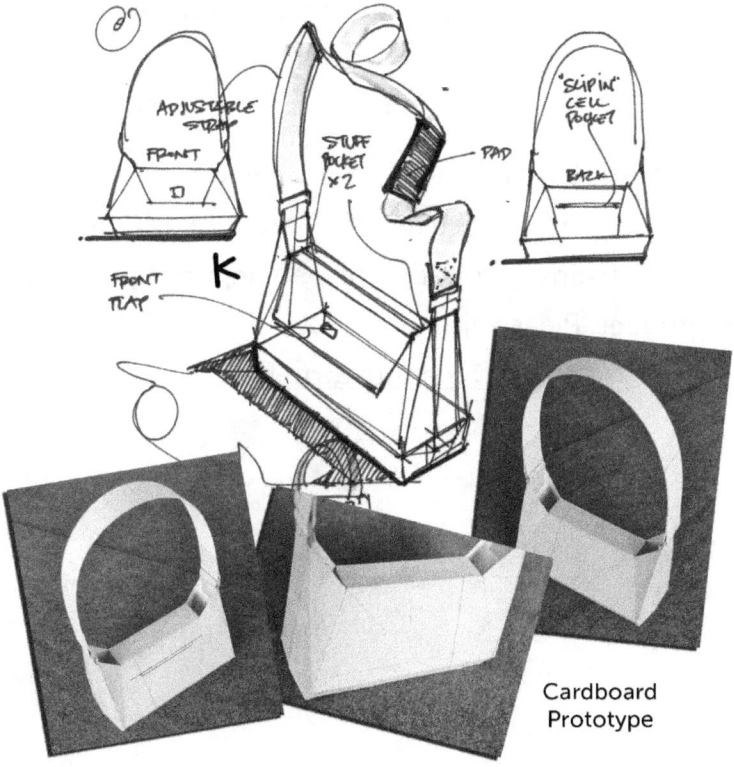

Cardboard Prototype

If you're interested in hosting a bringstorm workshop or presentation, or if you want to share how the bringstorm process has supercharged your people, your process, and your product. Please visit:

<u>www.bringstorm.com</u>

References

"A Quote by Bill Murray." Goodreads. Accessed July 22, 2019. https://www.goodreads.com/quotes/6472665-the-more-relaxed-you-are-the-better-you-are-at.

"Aubrey De Grey Quotes." BrainyQuote. Accessed July 22, 2019. https://www.brainyquote.com/authors/aubrey_de_grey.

"Carlos Gracie, Jr. Quote." A. Accessed July 22, 2019. https://www.azquotes.com/quote/757072.

Covey, Stephen R. *Seven Habits of Highly Effective People*. Provo, UT: Steven R. Covey & Associates, 1986.

Gregorio, Jay. "Start With Why Simon Sinek TED Talk." YouTube. October 10, 2016. Accessed July 22, 2019. https://www.youtube.com/watch?v=kOC4xcCxnzg.

"Important Things with Demetri Martin." IMDb. Accessed July 21, 2019. https://www.imdb.com/title/tt1118038/episodes?season=2.

"Important Things with Demetri Martin." IMDb. Accessed July 22, 2019. https://www.imdb.com/title/tt1118038/episodes.

"Just Enough Is More: Exhibition on Milton Glaser." Glyphic. February 07, 2019. Accessed July 22, 2019. https://type.fans/just-enough-is-more-exhibition-on-milton-glaser/.

"Maddman: The Steve Madden Story." IMDb. December 01, 2017. Accessed July 22, 2019. https://www.imdb.com/title/tt2987718/.

"The Black Album." Spotify. January 01, 2003. Accessed July 22, 2019. https://open.spotify.com/album/4FWvo9oS4gRgHtAwDwUjiO.

"The Founder." IMDb. Accessed July 22, 2019. https://www.imdb.com/title/tt4276820/fullcredits.

"The Tim Ferriss Show." Spotify. Accessed July 22, 2019. https://open.spotify.com/show/5qSUyCrk9KR69lEiXbjwXM.

Vonnegut, Kurt. "Slaughterhouse-Five: A Novel (Modern Library 100 Best Novels)." Amazon. January 12, 1999. Accessed July 21, 2019. https://www.amazon.com/Slaughterhouse-Five-Novel-Modern-Library-Novels/dp/0385333846.

www.ingramcontent.com/pod-product-compliance
Lightning Source LLC
Chambersburg PA
CBHW070655220526
45466CB00001B/446